LOVE

LOVE

10 Minutes a Day to Color Your Way

CHER KAUFMANN

The Countryman Press
A division of W. W. Norton & Company
Independent Publishers Since 1923

For information about permission to reproduce selections from
this book, write to Permissions, The Countryman Press,
500 Fifth Avenue, New York, NY 10110

For information about special discounts for bulk purchases, please
contact W. W. Norton Special Sales at specialsales@wwnorton.com
or 800-233-4830

The Countryman Press
www.countrymanpress.com

A division of W. W. Norton & Company, Inc.
500 Fifth Avenue, New York, NY 10110
www.wwnorton.com

978-1-58157-467-8 (pbk.)

10   9   8   7   6   5   4   3   2   1

To Mark, my love and best friend

INTRODUCTION

"A bird does not sing because it has an answer. It sings because it has a song." This Chinese proverb says as much about the nature of love as it does about the nature of the bird. Love soars, sings, whispers, and dances in every cell of our being. Love creates blankets of kindness and ribbons of appreciation to weave the fabric of the human condition. Love swirls in rapture and untangles discord. Perhaps sweet and simple at first glance, love is deeply complex. Love has more layers than the visible spectrum can reveal, and yet we all know love when we see it.

Through friendship, family, and romance, as well as pets and nature, love's waves of tenderness expose the vulnerability and strength contained therein. Artists and poets, philosophers and spiritual leaders, have put love on display through ceremony and exhibition. The greatest imprint of love, however, is the fluttering joy that hastens our heartbeats and fills us to brimming.

How to use this book

- Feel the love at any time—morning, afternoon, or night—with reflections in these pages.
- You may find the book helpful to read at your leisure in small, 10-minute blocks. You may reflect and contemplate the important messages any time.
- You can find calm by coloring the pages provided that are paired with passages and inspirational quotes. Use this activity as a relaxing coloring meditation.
- Use the lined pages for fun, compelling prompts to help you see through the eyes of your heart.
- Blank pages also contain simple drawing prompts for your moments of artistic creativity.
- Randomly open to a page to see what insights you might gain on a given day.

Love is the only Gold

— Alfred Lord Tennyson

*"Only from the heart
can you touch the sky."*

—Rumi

Heart Opener

The body is a wonderful communicator of your inner feelings and thoughts. Your posture tells everyone the kind of day you are having and the level of confidence you carry. It has been proven that keeping your head down and rounding your shoulders forward can put excess pressure on your neck and shoulders, but did you know it can also put pressure on your heart? Compression down on the upper rib cage contracts blood flow and oxygen flow to the lungs and heart. Opening and expanding the chest can help open the heart.

Try lying down flat on your back with a towel rolled up underneath the length of your spine, allowing your arms to be open and relaxed, palms up. This gentle support will make room for your shoulders to roll back and be supported by the floor. Breathe easily and effortlessly. In and out. No rush—just you and your breath. Notice if your head is resting on the center back of the skull, where it will be most supported. Relax in this pose for as little as 5 minutes before you leave the house, and again when you return home, for soothing and amazing results.

What is your idea of a heart hug?

Draw a picture of you with your heart as big as your body—make it wonderful, beautiful, and important!

What is your favorite song that instantly makes your heart feel more free and available? How does it open your heart?

*"Wisdom is knowing we are all One.
Love is what it feels like and
Compassion is what its acts like."*

—Ethan Walker III

WISE HEART

In the Five Element Theory of Chinese Medicine, which uses aspects of the natural world to describe attributes of people, the heart is often linked to the characteristics of fire. Fire is warm and brings light to darkness. Fire flickers like a candle and burns long and bright in a bonfire. Fire is magical; it creates the spark in your eyes, your spontaneous giggle that froths up like effervescent bubbles popping in the air. It is being in love with life and awed by the world around you. Think of the feeling of when you create something wonderful and you cannot wait to share it with someone you love. This moment is your passion, your desire, your heart—your fire! And when you give someone something artistic, you are giving them a little bit of your heart, a little bit of your fire.

Having this energy can mean you are sensitive to the emotions of people around you. After all, being in love with life can also mean being very aware of it. Hearts are meant to be open and experience life, but it is also very important to protect this precious heart of yours. An open heart does not mean an exposed heart. A wise heart is always open, yet mindful.

Love can wash through you at any time, any where, even when simply watching a high school band, a team winning a game, children putting on a show, or one stranger helping another. When was the last time you felt a strong sense of love from observing a group working together or an individual opening their heart to another?

Every heartbeat purrs an infinite capacity to love.

THERE IS NO LIMIT TO THE POWER OF Loving

-John Morton

"To love oneself is the beginning of a lifelong romance."

—Oscar Wilde

Inspire Through Love

A guru once suggested that I keep all my personal, important, spiritual experiences to myself because it can lead to jealousy in others. I was surprised to hear this statement. He meant that not all experiences are meant to be shared; some are for my heart alone. While I understood his sentiment, I also felt that human vitality has a need, a *desire*, to be inspired and connected by the golden thread of potential and possibility. Hearing what is possible can sometimes open a door you were unaware of on your own. When you share with love, awe, and purity, the vibration is easy to connect to. Listen with curiosity and share with love, and the experiences you have will reflect your inspiration. Release any expectations to have others feel what you feel, think what you think, or say what you say. Love will find a way to inspire you and them.

"Love is the greatest refreshment in life."

—Pablo Picasso

DON'T FORGET TO LOVE YOURSELF

— SOREN KIERKEGAARD

INSIDE OUT

A dear friend, teacher, and yoga instructor once shared the message of learning from the inside out. In many cultures, she explained, people develop trust and love from outside of themselves and learn to bring it inward through what is seen as acceptable or expected. However, if you learn from the *inside*, by listening to your heart, the truth of who you are and your experience of life will always come from the foundation of love. Love from your innermost being, the divinity of your beautiful soul, will always outshine troubles and doubts from the outside world. Following your personal truth, listening with a compassionate ear, seeking good in others, and learning to set healthy boundaries are a few of the ways in which your inside heart will shine out. If you ask your heart to speak from the inside out, what message do you hear? What voice of graciousness fills your ears and leaves your lips? What amazing person do you want to be today? What would you accomplish today if you lived from the inside out?

I listen to the gentle messages my heart shares with me and I respond.

One thing I know deep in my heart about love is . . .

I took a DEEP Breath and LISTENED TO THE OLD Bray OF MY HEART. I AM. I AM. I AM

– SYLVIA PLATH

"Love . . . it surrounds every being and extends slowly to embrace all that shall be."

—Khalil Gibran

"Your vision will become clear only when you can look into your own heart."

—Carl Jung

THE CATERPILLAR AND THE BUTTERFLY

There once was a caterpillar who was so curious to see above the grass that she climbed to the top of a long stalk. She rested a long while and had strange dreams of colors and wind moving around her body in ways she had not experienced before. She dreamt of lightness and freedom, of tranquility, and leaving something behind her. She awoke from her slumber feeling different, with a soft goodbye mixed with the liberation of rebirth, inspired by the whisper of an uncharted, exciting future yet to be revealed. She slowly stretched, a feeling that was new and vibrant. She paused, she strengthened, and she unfolded. She breathed in the wind and the wind responded. It carried her above the grass. The wind taught her to travel lightly and to drink from the colors of many petals. This—*this*—was the greatest gift of love: following her heart, living the potential, transforming, and understanding that there was no loss—only a connection to much more.

"Love makes your soul crawl out from its hiding place."

—Zora Neale Hurston

If you were a butterfly, what would you look like? Use words, draw a picture, or do both. What would the first flower you visited look like?

Kindness feeds
the love within.

"If only you could sense how important you are to the lives of those you meet; how important you can be to people you may never even dream of. There is something of yourself that you leave at every meeting with another person."

—Fred Rogers

Love is but the DISCOVERY of Ourselves in Others and the Delight in the Recognition

—Alexander Smith

Have you ever had a chance encounter that inspired you in some way? It doesn't have to be big—sometimes the smallest things make the biggest impact (like a smile!).

*"There is no remedy for love
but to love more."*

—Henry David Thoreau

MY HEAVEN, MY SKY

My great-uncle had a nickname for my great-aunt. He would call her *Mi Cielo*, which translates from Spanish as "my heaven" or "my sky." They saw a lot of changes in their lifetime—technology, families, cars, jobs, travel, and responsibilities—and it wasn't always perfect by any means. Although never formally trained as a nurse, my great-aunt was a born caretaker who has lovingly tended to many family members. My great-uncle enjoyed the guitar and singing with his sisters in the backyard and at family gatherings and celebrations. Family was always around them in one form or another; immediate and extended, sisters, brothers, cousins. "Where is *mi cielo*?" he would ask. There could be a sea of people, waves of family all around, and yet my great-uncle always asked where my great-aunt was. I felt she acted as a buoy or an anchor, a place of solid ground, a touchstone he could count on no matter where he was or how many people surrounded him. It was a very special love. The night he passed away, the phone rang in the middle of the night. There was no one there when my great-aunt answered. Perhaps it was heaven, saying good-bye to his sky.

If you could describe the love you feel for another person in one word or a short phrase (without using the word "love"), what would you say? Make it fun, silly, sincere, divine, deep, crazy, light—get creative!

"A kiss is a rosy dot over the 'i' of loving."

—Cyrano de Bergerac

Create Your Own Love Poem
use the letters below to begin each line.

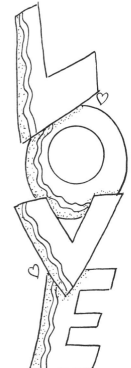

LET Yourself

Be Drawn

BY THE STRONGER

Pull OF THAT

WHICH

YOU

Truly Love

— RUMI

HO'OPONOPONO

Ho'oponopono (ho-oh-pono-pono) is a Hawaiian method of traditional healing. Healing is achieved by repeating the following statements over and over again in a sincere way, and taking absolute responsibility for what is being viewed as "wrong" or "bad." (Yes, even if you feel it has nothing to do with you. You do not even need to be near the issue you are thinking about—it could be across the street or across the world.) The idea is to acknowledge the shadow part of ourself, the part we reject or judge in others. When this is healed, the issue is dissolved for all involved.

With an open mind, a sincere heart, and a loving intention, think of something in the world that needs more love and repeat it to yourself and to the thought you are holding:

I love you.

Please forgive me.

I am sorry.

Thank you.

There is nothing more you need to do. There is no "fixing" or adding more words—simply the intention of complete forgiveness and love from one beautiful heart to another. Try it. Repeat this for as long as the issue remains.

"I love you. Please forgive me. I am sorry. Thank you."
Draw a picture of a healed heart filled with
something wonderful (patterns, colors, stars,
more hearts, smiley faces, colors, etc.).

"Love is the beauty of the soul."

—Saint Augustine

THE ROSE

Have you ever been to the flower shop looking for that perfect rose? You know the one: with flawless, velvety petals; an aroma that lasts for days; a strong, sturdy stem; thornless; and a color rich enough to paint a canvas with a single drop. I used to think these flowers were the ones to seek and purchase, and that all others were somehow less than—until I discovered the carnation, with its fluttery petals and a light, fresh scent that held up for a month; and baby's breath, with its teeny-tiny, delicate white blooms on spindle-like stems amid the long-leaf grasses. I realized that, while the ideal rose may be what I thought I wanted, beauty comes in a vast variety of shapes, sizes, and fragrances. Next to a beautiful flower, it is love that fills me—not the smell of a single, perfect rose. Love is perfect in all of its expressions—but the best expression is the one I choose to have in return.

I allow the gifts of
nature to replenish
my senses of awe,
appreciation,
and love.

Color

Design

Add on

Create

Draw your favorite flower (or flowers) and color them.

With the
New Day
comes
New Strength
and
New Thoughts

-Eleanor
Roosevelt

YOU ARE LIGHT (REALLY!)

Your body is an amazingly complex, intricate machine of intelligence, energy, movement, and light. Did you know that you actually glow with light? Biophotons in your body produce light at the ultraviolet and low visible frequency range—they are much weaker in brightness than bioluminescence, but they glow nonetheless!

The energy that elicits change in your body comes from thoughts in your mind. This means that your body, in essence, "hears" every thought you have. Every brilliant idea, every happy inside giggle, every emotion that is processed. Within 90 seconds, they are felt completely by all of you. Negative self-talk in thought, word, action, or emotion is also "heard" by your entire being. You are not alone with your thoughts. Every organ, cell, particle, and wave of who you are either lights up your lights (literally) or dims them down with your thoughts, health, and well-being.

Today, keep in mind just how many loving thoughts your body hears and how many not-so-loving thoughts it hears. Try this: Take a deep breath in and imagine your lights getting brighter, pause, and gently breathe out. Let your lights glow, happy to be acknowledged. Breathe in again, expand your lights, pause, then breathe out, relax, and glow. Repeat. Be the light you are: glow, inspire, and be well.

"There are never enough I Love You's."

—Lenny Bruce

If you could see your body with happy lights all over it, what color would they be? Draw a picture (yes, stick figures are OK!). Draw yourself glowing from all your happy thoughts.

I love the smallest parts of myself as well as my whole being with compassion, gratitude, and adoration.

"To love and be loved is to feel the sun from both sides."

—David Viscott

YOUR HEART

Science has shown that the heart has an electrical field that emits a detectable frequency (ECG) 60 times stronger than brain waves measured with an electroencephalogram (EEG). The incredible power of the heart implies that it has a tangible energy field valuable to your well-being, and provides stability for your health. Your emotional vitality is deeply connected to your physical heart as well. It has been documented that anxiety can affect the rhythm of the heartbeat. This means that giving and receiving love is a crucial component to the healthy physical, emotional, and spiritual fulfillment of your life! Your physical heart will tell you when you need connections with people, animals, and nature, *and* when you need some time to recharge alone in peacefulness. Listen to the wisdom of this remarkable part of you: your fire, your heart, your love.

Finish this sentence: "My heart lets me know when I need to connect with others and when I need to recharge quietly by . . ."

Inspiration is love's gentle nudge to follow your heart.